Let's Play

and other things animals say

Contents

Alison Blank

OXFORD

Introduction

Think of all the things you say every day.

Want to play?

I'm hungry.

Be my friend.

Stay away!

Your words tell others what you want and how you feel. You also **communicate** without words. You:

All animals communicate. Unlike us, animals don't use words. They use sight, sound, touch and smell instead.

In this book you will discover some of the amazing ways that animals communicate with each other.

What do you think these animals are saying?

Frogs croak

Attracting a mate

It's a spring evening and, as the sun sets, you hear a croak by the pond. Then another croak and another. Soon the air is full of the noise of croaking. Croaking is the noise made by male frogs when they are trying to attract female frogs.

What do you do when you want attention?

To make that croaking sound a frog fills a **sac** in his throat with air. Then he makes the sac **vibrate** to make a noise.

In warm weather, male crickets chirp by rubbing their wings together. That chirp tells a female cricket, “I’m over here”.

Bees dance

Giving directions

Bees gather **nectar** and **pollen** from the inside of flowers. Then they return to the beehive with this food. At the hive, a bee will tell the other bees where it found the flowers. How? It dances.

Without using words, how would you give directions?

The dance shows the other bees how far away to fly and in what **direction**.

When an ant finds food, it returns home leaving a **chemical trail** along the ground. Other ants then follow the smell of those chemicals all the way to the food.

Snakes puff up

Stay away!

Some animals make themselves look scary or tough when they are scared. This is a warning to "Stay away!"

Some people are scared of snakes. But snakes get scared too! When an owl swoops down from the sky, it's the snake that feels scared. That's because owls like to eat snakes. So how do snakes defend themselves? Some puff their heads up so they look big and mean.

If you don't want someone to know you are scared, what do you do?

Rattlesnakes say "Stay away!" differently. They rattle their tail to make a threatening sound. If that doesn't work, they bite their enemy.

An owl puffs up its feathers to look bigger and meaner. It says, "Don't mess with me!"

Birds strut

Being noticed

Many male birds have spectacular feathers or unusual colours to attract attention.

To **impress** a female, the peacock fans out his tail feathers and struts up and down. His tail has over 200 feathers. Each tail feather is decorated with a beautiful pattern which looks like an eye.

When a peacock shows off his feathers, he is saying "Look at me!"

How do you say, "Be my friend"?

The blue-footed booby gets a female's attention by showing off his handsome blue feet.

Lemurs smell

Marking territory

Lemurs say it with smell. They have **glands** under their arms which give off a strong scent. A lemur smears this scent onto his tail. He then waves his tail around. This smell warns other lemurs from other groups, "I've been here. Stay away!"

How could you leave a message that says "I've been here"?

Wild lemurs are only found on the island of Madagascar, off the coast of Africa. They live together in groups of 30 and defend their territory from other lemurs.

A mountain lion marks his **territory** by **urinating** on piles of dirt or leaves. The smell **signals** to other animals, “This is my territory. Keep out!”

Monkeys howl

Keeping in touch

Howler monkeys live in the tree tops. All day long, troops of howlers move through the forest. They eat fruit, groom each other and make noise.

Howler monkeys live in Central and South America. They are one of the loudest animals in the world.

Howler monkeys roar, grunt and howl so loudly that their sounds can travel over 3 kilometres. What are they saying? Most of the time, they are letting other troops know where they are.

Hyenas love to talk! They howl, squeal and cackle. People call them 'laughing hyenas' because of the cackling sound they make.

How do you let someone know where you are?

Dolphins whistle

Keeping together

A dolphin whistles, squeaks, moans and clicks by moving air underneath its **blowhole**. Dolphins make these noises to communicate with each other and to find food.

Do you and a friend or parent have a special signal?

Dolphins each have their own special whistle sounds. Sometimes, a baby dolphin swims too far from its mother. Then the mother will whistle, “Where are you?” The baby will whistle, “Here I am.”

Male humpback whales sing songs that can last up to 30 minutes at a time. They sing these songs during the breeding season to attract females.

Elephants rumble

Sending messages

An elephant can make at least 25 different calls with its throat and trunk. One call means: "Hello." Another call means: "Where are you?"

After a rest, a mother elephant says to her family, "Let's go."

Elephants also make a low rumbling sound that humans can't hear. However, other elephants can hear these sounds almost 10 kilometres away.

Scientists think that some animals, like these hippos, are able to predict natural disasters. That's because these animals can hear the low rumbles that tornadoes or earthquakes make.

How do you greet a friend you are happy to see?

What is your cat saying?

Do you have a pet cat? How well do you know your cat? Look at each picture and make a guess. What do you think the cats are saying? Check your answer below.

- ☐ **a)** "I want to learn to knit."
- ☐ **b)** "This is fun."
- ☐ **c)** "Get out of my way!"

- ☐ **a)** "I can't wait to read this book."
- ☐ **b)** "This is uncomfortable."
- ☐ **c)** "I don't like you paying attention to something that isn't me."

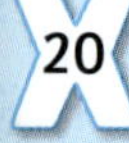

- a) "I'm trying to look scary because I'm afraid."
- b) "Brrr. I'm cold."
- c) "Want to play?"

- a) "I have an itch."
- b) "You're my friend."
- c) "I'm bored!"

Answers: 1b; 2c; 3a; 4b.

What is your dog saying?

Do you have a pet dog? How well do you know your dog? Look at each picture and make a guess. What do you think the dogs are saying? Check your answer below.

1

☐ **a)** “Want to play?”

☐ **b)** “Your highness, I bow before you.”

☐ **c)** “I think I dropped something.”

2

☐ **a)** “Don’t mess with me. I am really angry!”

☐ **b)** “I’m feeling a little upset.”

☐ **c)** “Like my teeth?”

3

- [ ] **a)** "I always lean to one side."
- [ ] **b)** "I didn't get that joke."
- [ ] **c)** "Did you hear that?"

4

- [ ] **a)** "Glad to meet you."
- [ ] **b)** "Please pay attention to me!"
- [ ] **c)** "It's over there."

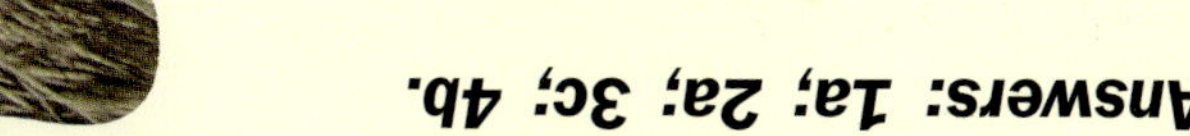

Glossary

blowhole	a hole in the top of a dolphin's head through which it breathes
chemical trail	the smell that some animals make to show the way from one place to another
communicate	to pass on information
direction	the way something is going
gland	an organ in a human or animal's body
impress	to make someone think something is very good
nectar	a sweet liquid in flowers that bees use to make honey
pollen	a yellow powder that you find inside flowers
sac	part of an animal's body that is shaped like a bag and contains air or water
signal	to give information, instructions or a warning
territory	the land that a person or an animal owns or uses
urinate	to get rid of the waste liquid that collects in the bladder
vibrate	to shake